© 2017 Will Jorden
All rights reserved. No portion of this book may be
without permission from the publisher, except as pe........u by U.S. copyright law.

Dedicated to all the F's in my life.

(Family, Friends, Failures, Fears)

Will's Disclaimer

About the author and how this book came into being.

This is not a Self-Help book.

Ch 1. It must suck to be you.
Your life, your problem.
Defining the problem.
The rise of a movement.

Ch 2. What it means to be worthless.
Where does happiness even come from?
Karma is BS
You're unique, just like everyone else..
Your ugliness is more than skin deep.
A brief note on sympathy

Ch 3. How you became so worthless.
Blame your ancestors.
Be kind rewind.
Right up the bumhole.
Pleasure without regard to consequences.
You're Mediocre.

Ch 4. Your personal worthlessness.
You're the reason your life sucks.
You'll never be as cool as those you compare yourself too.
You're replaceable.
You'll never find success.

Ch 5. You've been setting yourself up for failure.
You annihilated your natural born instinct.
Sowing the seeds of your demise.
To settle down is to settle.
Responsibility and excuses.
Procrastination.

Ch 6. Hard Truths.
"The Pussy Generation"-Clint Eastwood
Ch-ch-ch-changes.
Accepting failure into your life.
Living with worthlessness.

Ch 7. The plan of inaction.
Don't bother trying to change.

The malfeasance of self confidence.
Hakuna Matata.
Finalizing change.

Ch 8. Things to remember on your journey nowhere.
The Hierarchy of Needs.
The indifference of the universe.
Sh*t Happens.
It's too late to die young.

Ch 9. Do whatever you want.
Predestination.
Reward Yourself.
Take control of your life.
Effort is discomfort.

Ch 10. Taming your life.
Strategy Vs Tactics.
Be as successful as you want to be.
Procrastination.
Unmotivated Motivation.
Laugh
The Most Important Lesson In This Book

In Conclusion

Will's Disclaimer

Don't be stupid. This is a book you got off the internet, take all the advice and information you gleam from these pages with a grain of salt. If you need psychiatric help this book is probably the last thing you should read.

Also, don't take this book with actual grains of salt. The human body can't support that level of sodium intake. Death may occur in some cases.

About the author and how this book came into being.

What type of mean and miserable millennial would write a book calling people out on their worthlessness? One with experience that's who. I have personally seen the horrendous effects of living with worthlessness because I am worthless. It's something I've struggled with all my life but I've learned to accept it. Learning to accept your worthlessness and live in harmony with it is what this book is all about.

If you want to know more about myself you can read my books <u>I'm Worthless And I Know It Volumes 1 and 2.</u> These books feature multiple short stories from my life that depict what a worthless individual I am. It features my life's most embarrassing and regretful moments that any onlooker will find delight in. But for now I'd like to tell you the story of how this book came into being.

In 2016 I had been working at a Los Angeles indoor trampoline park for 4 years. I found myself at 30 years old working a minimum wage, part time job alongside teenagers to keep my finances afloat. At this time my acting career was as prosperous as a degree in Liberal Studies, which I also have.

Every day I'd be at work and see my coworkers come in, they were children half my age and that goes for most of management as well. They would be smiling, retelling the stories of their youthful adventures to In and Out for some hamburgers or that crazy party that was interrupted by their curfew.

They were full of life and excited about what the future would bring them, those foolish mortals. They made me sick. They had no concept of what life is like outside of their parents womb or that life is all a twisted game meant to give you just enough hope to keep you from ending it yourself.

I had enough and decided I needed to educate them for their benefit on the way life really is. Their education began with a dry erase board in the break room where I would write my words of wisdom. I put up quotes such as:

- "It's not too late to die young."
- "Everyone makes mistakes... and you're one of them."
- "Live with no regrets. You've probably ruined your life by now anyway."
- "You're not as cool as the people you compare yourself to"
- "You'll never reach your million dollar dream with your minimum wage worth ethic."
- "If I have to sugarcoat it for you, you're a bitch."
- "You'll be fatter next year."
- "Hope is what people do on their deathbed."

These quotes would springboard conversations between us as we stood around and made sure the little kids didn't stick their boogers on the trampolines. My young coworkers were open to my life experiences and became quick learners. I was pleased with their progress and they encouraged me to turn my lessons into a book so that I could help influence a generation of worthless snowflake individuals. This is that book.

This is not a Self-Help book.

The problem with self-help books is that they inspire people. That's the last thing you want because if you're inspired you'll have further to fall when you fail. And you will fail, you're a failure it's what you do. Your best hope is self enlightenment but that ain't sunshine and rainbows. It means accepting yourself for the worthless parasitic organism that you are.

Throughout this book you'll learn what it means to be worthless and exactly why you're worthless. You know some of why you're worthless but even Yoda was a student once. Through my vast knowledge and experience I'll guide you through the process of discovering for yourself the depths of your failures and inadequacies. During this process you'll learn:

- What it means to be worthless.
- How you became worthless.
- How your worthlessness manifests itself.
- How you've been setting yourself up for failure your whole life.
- The malfeasance of self confidence.
- Why you shouldn't concern yourself with higher functions of humanity.
- How to live with yourself after knowing how worthless you are.
- And the most important lesson to be revealed in the end.

Now prepare yourself for a journey into the depths of your personal worthlessness. There will be times when you'll want to fight me and tell me that you aren't worthless but I will guide you through it. In addition I'll work you through the top ways of living with you personal brand of worthlessness so that you can maximize your safe space.

My hope in writing this book is that you'll have the courage to see the worthlessness in yourself and point out the worthlessness in others. Pass this knowledge on and let's begin a conversation so that we can deal with our first world problems in an open manner.

Ch 1. It must suck to be you.

      Human life may or may not be meaningless in the grand scheme of things but your life sure is. The notion that you're worthless and you know it is one that you probably found humorous when you read the title of this book. You didn't take it seriously because to suddenly accept your life doesn't possess objective value or meaning would throw you into a existential crisis.

      That's part of the goal of this book, to break you down until you've freed yourself of all your self worth and thus found enlightenment in emptiness. By separating yourself from will and desire you will in return reduce your suffering. If you don't have anything then you can't lose anything and if you don't want anything then you can't be disappointed when you don't get anything.

Knowledge is contained through perspective thus it is through our interpretations that can we give knowledge meaning. In order for you to accept the Will of Nothingness you must first change your perspective. To do this we will judge the world as it is, that it ought not to be, and as it ought to be that doesn't or will never exist.

Your life, your problem.

I'm going to guess that from a lifetime of worthlessness you have somehow managed to retain some sense of self worth. This is probably the case because like most people you have a nasty habit of giving meaning to your suffering. You tell yourself you're suffering because you're working hard for your future or for someone else. Perhaps your suffering comes from being the innocent victim or comes from not finding the pleasures you think you deserve.

You cling to the meaning you give your suffering because if your suffering has meaning than that must mean your life has meaning. But there's no meaning to your life. You weren't born with meaning and you certainly haven't found any in the decades you've been alive.

It's true that you were dealt a lousy hand in life and that nothing has gone your way. Despite all of that, you're still capable of greatness and yet you've squandered it. As people we tend to judge ourselves by what we're capable of rather than what we've accomplished.

If you were to look at your life from someone else's perspective what would you see? Probably not much because in defiance of how hard you've worked you haven't gotten anywhere.

It doesn't matter what's in your heart or your head, the thing that matters is your actions and everyone has the right to judge you based on them. But their judgement doesn't matter, you know the depths and the intimacies of your worthlessness.

Defining the problem.

Before we move any further we first need to define what worthlessness is. For starters you won't be remembered after your death. What have you done in your life that has made you memorable? You didn't invent the internet or the first airplane. You weren't the first person to step on the moon or come up with the theory of evolution. You haven't done anything in your life and you won't have a statue or pyramid built in your honor when you die.

In fact you haven't given anything back to society. You're essentially a parasite on the ball-sack of humanity. You work so that your employer can become wealthy, you spend your money on things that make other people rich, and you consume goods that are sucking earth's natural resources dry.

But you're not worthless because you haven't done anything or because you haven't contributed, you're worthless because you haven't lived up to your potential. That's the primary focus of worthlessness in this book and something you'll learn to accept and live with by the time you've finished reading it.

The rise of a movement.

All self help books would have you imagine yourself as someone who's capable of limitless achievements. Sadly all that does is set you up for limitless disappointment when you fail to achieve anything. I want you to achieve victory through being honest with yourself and understanding that achievement won't bring you happiness.

Life is meaningless. William Shakespeare described life best in his Scottish play (that shall not be named because of the curse):

Out, out, brief candle!
Life's but a walking shadow, a poor player
That struts and frets his hour upon the stage
And then is heard no more; it is a tale
Told by an idiot, full of sound and fury,
Signifying nothing.

The universe is so vast and complex that our consciousness can't comprehend it. You're born into this universe isolated and without purpose. Society will tell you that's untrue and you do have purpose you just need to conform into society's image and find it. People that claim to have found purpose are delusional and full of themselves, they're telling you to perpetuate the lie they tell themselves every day.

If someone can be honest and acknowledge the meaninglessness of life they can then be free of the burden society would have you place upon yourself.

Ch 2. What it means to be worthless.

We'll go into why you're a worthless human being over the next three chapters but we first need to lay some ground work. Your human desires are futile, directionless, and illogical as are all the actions of mankind.

The world is your representation and as Einstein said, "Man can indeed do what he wants, but he cannot will what he wants." The "will" that he is talking about is the same will in the term "free will." It doesn't matter if you believe in the concept of having free will and the ability to choose different courses of actions or you believe everything is predetermined. What we can agree on is that you never chose to have free will or to not.

If free will does exists then it was forced upon you and we can derive from this that will is a blind force controlling everything about who you are and what you do. This means that your worthlessness comes from you and how you deal with your worthlessness is upon you as well.

Where does happiness even come from?

Who are you all by yourself? Are you whole, nourished, and soulful or do you look to a significant other to "complete you?" The latter is actually pretty smart as you'll never be able to fill all the holes in your life without the inclusion of others, especially when it comes to happiness. At least 40% of your happiness should come from the manipulation of others. The most efficient way to do this is by being overly dramatic and gaining sympathy in your search for false validation.

The other 60% comes from two separate but equal types of happiness; Low Grade Happiness (LGH) and High Grade Happiness (HGH). LGH is comprised of cheap thrills and guilty pleasures where as HGH is happiness that you have to work for, such as accomplishments.

Despite it's name HGH isn't any better than LGH. You're just lead to believe that by society. Eating a candy bar from a vending machine will bring you as much happiness as going through the process of making a candy bar and eating it. Getting likes on a social media post is equal to the pleasure you get from winning an achievement award despite how much more effort one takes over the other.

Society tells you you'll never be "truly happy" (whatever that means) unless you accomplish something great. But let's be honest you're fine with your happiness coming from cheap thrills and guilty pleasures, it's what you're addicted to. Happiness isn't even real, if anything it's fleeting, it's not our normal resting state. Happiness is the absence of pain and suffering, which are our normal resting states.

Karma is BS

kar*ma

ˈkärmə/

noun

noun: karma

1 (in Hinduism and Buddhism) the sum of a person's actions in this and previous states of existence, viewed as deciding their fate in future existences.

- informal

destiny or fate, following as effect from cause.

So let me get this straight, my current actions and "previous states of existence" (whatever that means) decide what will happen to me in the future? This has been interpreted as if I'm a good little boy/girl good things will happen to me down the road.

This is BS, the concept of karma was developed by a group of dicks who wanted the sheeple (sheep people) to be nice to them. And they wanted this without doing anything in return except tell them that since you were nice to me nice things will happen to you at an unknown date. This is crazy, doing good work will not magically attract good things to you and anyone who tells you otherwise is manipulating you, end of story.

You're unique, just like

everyone else.

You're unique and I wouldn't question you on that, quite the contrary. You're an interesting human specimen, as no one else on a planet of 7+Billion people has your combination of imperfections. And like all goods with imperfections you're not as valuable as others who have a different set of imperfections.

There are people born more special than you who were destined to find success through their higher I.Q. If you're an engineer with the average I.Q. of 100 you'll never be able to compete with an engineer who has an I.Q. of 140. And it won't matter if you work harder, they'll work smarter, that's life. Others will use their beauty or a combination of that and their higher I.Q. to advance past you in your chosen field.

I work at an indoor trampoline park in Los Angeles and it enrages me every time a semi famous rapper comes in. I couldn't care less about the rapper, it's his entourage that upsets me. On average a rapper comes in with a ratio of 5 hot girls to every one guy. These boys do nothing but stroke the rapper's ego; they laugh at his jokes, applaud him for nothing, and serve as his general amusement. The women have it even easier, they just look pretty.

The girls aren't just pretty, they're smoking hot! But trust me, I've tried to talk to them and they have absolutely no personality despite how good their selfies are for their Instagram accounts. These women are getting a free ride to the high life without having to do anything, meanwhile you and I are living pay check to pay check as we accomplish nothing and slowly die alone.

Your ugliness is more than skin deep.

There's this little thing called "the crap gap." It's the difference between what a person says they want and what their actual behavior suggests. For instance a person will tell you they want to be healthy at the same time they're drinking a soda and eating three Happy Meals with extra ketchup. The cause of the crap gap is pretty simple.

The world without is a reflection of the world within. Despite what you tell yourself and others there's a filthy, dirty, sinful monster in your soul and it will manifest itself through your actions. It could be gluttony, lust, greed, rage, and so on. This inner demon isn't connected to your mind, your mind is processed through social norms where as this demon isn't. Deep within you lies a bitter, cynical, negative, sickly, and ugly person with an infinite supply of bad ideas waiting to manifest itself to the world outside of you.

People who have poor skin are often unhealthy eaters, this is because the world without is a reflection of the world within. The same goes for your ugly actions. So the next time your significant other takes care of you through your seasonal depression and you return the favor by cheating on them with a 21 year old jobless punk in a boy band who lives in his mom's garage smoking weed all day, know that it's a reflection of the ugliness that's inside you. (You know who you are.)

A brief note on sympathy

Think you'll get sympathy because of your worthlessness? Fat chance. Here's a little lesson from retired law enforcement officer and legendary fire arms instructor Clint Smith. If you want to find sympathy look for it in the dictionary. You'll find it somewhere in-between "Shit" and "Syphilis," right where it belongs. So quit your whining and accept your worthlessness.

Ch 3. How you became so worthless.

Your worthlessness isn't something you acquired over night, the inklings of it are in your genes. You're like an angst filled teenager in the X-Men comics. You've been pushed to the breaking point and your mutant power has showed itself in the form of super worthlessness.

But in order to know where you're going you first have to know where you've been and how you've gotten to this point. That's not to say with this knowledge you can rid yourself of your worthlessness, but knowledge is power.

Blame your ancestors.

Way back in the caveman days a group of primitive peoples came across their first Sabortooth Tiger. Some of them wanted to pet the pretty kitty while others hesitated. Those who tried to pet the 800 pound cat were mauled to death and those that hesitated lived long enough to pass their genes down to the next generation. Do this for one or two generations and it won't have much effect on humanity. But after 6 million years of human evolution this cycle begins to shape how we behave when only the fearful live long enough to reproduce. Keep in mind that civilization as we know it has been around for 6,000 years and up until then the world was much more dangerous.

Bravery isn't an evolutionary trait and neither is motivation. So it's no wonder that we find we aren't motivated to want to do difficult, uncertain, or scary things. Fear is the mother of all safety. It's the easy and safe things that we're willing to do because our brains believe them to be the least likely to get us killed.

When your brain is scared it's scared, it doesn't matter if you're scared of a Sabortooth Tiger or talking to your crush, the emotion is the same and your brain reacts the same.

There will be more on this in Chapter 10 but for now it's important that you understand why you've struggled to act outside of your comfort zone.

Be kind rewind.

Let me talk to my fellow Millennials for a minute. Did we have an awesome childhood or what?! The 90's were an excellent time to grow up, aside from it helping make us the worthless individuals we are today.

We played outside in relative safety during a time when, if you wanted to know what your friends were doing you could either ask your parents to use the phone or you could ride your bike to their house and hope they weren't eating dinner.

I'm not sure what you girls did during this time but us boys played with our Super Soakers, Nerf guns, and built forts with whatever we could find. When we were inside we polished our participation trophies, played with Legos, the Nintendo 64, or we watched movies on VHS like <u>Space Jam</u> and <u>The Goonines</u>. And our <u>Teenage Mutant Ninja Turtles</u> weren't giant grotesque monsters as Michael Bay would have you believe.

Not only did we have the greatest toys and movies of

all time but we had parents who were less likely to spank us and more likely to buy us those toys than any other generation in history. We looked forward to getting older and by the time the turn of the century happened life was becoming more fantastical.

Dial up internet was becoming a thing of the past, Pluto was still every underdog's favorite planet, and we were getting used to a new President with a Texan accent. And while every literate kid anxiously awaited the release of the 5th Harry Potter book we were beginning those awkward teenage years.

One Tuesday morning my mom dropped me off at school, our Honda Odyssey had automatic doors and they embarrassed me. As kids I knew were walking by I pretended to close the door manually but as the sound of the door's motor grinded away I grew more embarrassed as I realized I wasn't fooling anyone.

That was pretty much the extent of my adolescent world, trying not to embarrass myself but all that changed an hour later when American Airlines Flight 11 crashed into the World Trade Center. And as other planes crashed and buildings fell the young students around me began to draw wild conclusions from what little information we had. The day progressed and the school was flooded with rumors that only grew more outlandish by the hour as the anxiety and the fear grew. I vividly remember one kid sobbing as he stumbled passed me in the hallway, he was rambling that terrorist will be targeting us any minute because they hate kids here in Oklahoma.

This was the first time I ever realized kids had their own cell phones. Those lucky students had the chance to call home and talk to their parents and make sure everything was okay and that the terrorists hadn't gotten them. We had no idea what was going on, we were were suddenly thrown into the real world. We were used to helicopter moms who hovered over us ready to pick us up every time we fell.

For those Millennials' who were too young to lose their childhood that day they only had to wait a few years for the worst financial crises since the Great Depression. And they watched as their parents lost their jobs and their homes or at least stressed over the uncertainty.

From having such awesome childhoods, reality of the real world hit us pretty hard. It's a big part of how we're identified as Millennials. We love our nostalgia, our feel good laws, and our safe spaces because we want to go back to that innocent time when we were kids. It's part of what makes us worthless as we're too scared to take chances or leave home.

In 2014, 45% of millennials (who's ages range from 18 to 34) still lived in their parents house and only 1% were moving out each year. How pathetic are we? And it's our patheticness that leads us on to the next section.

Right up the bumhole.

There are two demographics bending us over and screwing us into patheticness. The first one comes from the lies of the generations that came before us who gave us catchy slogans like, "Be cool, stay in school." This caused us to be the most educated generation, but we're also the largest generation which has lead to more potential educated workers than jobs for educated people. For us, the college diploma is what the high school diploma used to be.

For older generations, college was a place to learn how to think critically and question the world so that they could contribute in ways no one had thought of. College is now a place where you go to find a career and that's not working too well in the current job market. The Pew Research Center tells us that 40% of minimum wage workers have college degrees and 40% of unemployed workers are millennials.

We're also entering the workforce and adulthood with more debt than any other generation. College graduates in 1993 who borrowed money had, on average, $9,000 in student loan debt. According to The Huffington Post that number has risen and currently 70% of graduating students have over $30,000 in debt. It's no wonder we want free college education and a higher minimum wage. And according to Psychology Today we have the highest levels of clinical anxiety, stress, and depression compared to any other generation at the same age.

Yeah we're screwed. Now that we're older and we realize that real life doesn't give participation trophies and is filled with more pollution and corruption than we can hope to clean up. So the old folk screwed us, so what, they're not the only ones.

We've been making horrible decisions all on our own. For starters we grew up idolizing those who didn't give a flying flute. The coolest kids in school where the ones who didn't care about anything and everyone made fun of the "try hards." This has persisted into adulthood as we don't want to work hard. We make excuses and complain we can't find jobs but in all honesty we should be complaining that we can't find jobs we WANT to do. Not since the industrial revolution of WW2 have there been so many blue collar jobs available but Millennials would rather live with their parents, and we are.

Another way we are screwing ourselves comes from our

short sightedness. Look no further than the fact that my generation spends more on latte's each year than we do saving for retirement. I wonder how that's going to work in 40+ years.

Pleasure without regard to consequences.

Research suggests that people are more likely to ignore a larger payout in the future if they can get an immediate reward. In fact people are willing to ignore just about anything for a quick payout and that goes for consequences too. Admit it, you're guilty of playing a few too many rounds of Call of Duty instead of studying for that test which will make or break your grade. You've skipped dentist appointments, family gathering, and work shifts all so you could have an immediate pleasure of some kind.

This is a huge part of what's made you worthless. Your disinterests in exercise and love of junk food has made you over-weight and probably taken years off your life. If you haven't scared off the opposite sex with your looks then the STD's you got from having multiple sex partners will, which as well is enjoying immediate pleasures without regard to consequences.

You're not worthless because you want to have fun in life, you're worthless because your impulsiveness has left you an empty shell. Sure you'll feel bad when your significant other confronts you about cheating on them but really you're just upset that you have to deal with the situation you got yourself into. And the same goes for anytime your pleasurable past actions catch up with you. Of course you'll find some way to make yourself the victim but it won't deny the fact that you're a worthless individual.

You're Mediocre.

The first step on the road to acceptance is acknowledging that you have a problem. That problem is mediocrity and you've allowed it into every facet of your life as you've become complacent over time. That's not to say you don't have standards, you just don't have the will power to uphold them.

Your standards for health aren't being met because you lack discipline when it comes to getting exercise, eating healthy, and eating the correct portions. The music and television you enjoy is garbage. And the people you've allowed into your life are also subpar as they don't uphold the same standards you'd like to have for yourself.

It's been said that a person is the average of the 5 people they come in contact with the most. If you were surrounded by successful people you'd be inspired to uphold your standards and reach for success. But that's beside the point as your lack of will power has led to a life of mediocrity.

You watch sports instead of participating, you don't create art or music and instead substitute it for the advertising based media produced by studio committees. But as far as you're concerned your life revolves around getting likes and internet followers. I can't think of anything that symbolizes mediocrity more than wanting people to like the picture you took of your Olive Garden salad, you worthless pile of trash.

Ch 4. Your personal worthlessness.

Every business has it's own brand. When you think of Apple you may associate them with seamless, over-priced, stolen innovation and you may think of Amazon as the most convenient thing since the inflatable sex doll.

And just as each fast food chain has their own brand every person has their own brand. Their own personal brand of worthlessness and that's what this chapter is devoted to.

Above everything else the number one thing that identifies as your personal brand comes from your ego. Your self-guided interests in your pursuit of pleasure and happiness drives your actions and inactions. It's also the ego that's the origin of all your pain, conflicts, and degradation of moral principles.

You're the reason your life sucks.

We've established that you were brought into this world under less than stellar conditions. Everyone is and yet some people make something of themselves. The Rock for example, Dwayne "The Rock" Johnson had a troubled childhood, from 13 to 17 he was arrested 9 times. He viewed himself as a failure but eventually made something of himself, which proves that if your life sucks it's your own fault.

There's a reason why you can't turn your life around. That reason is fear. You are the sum of your fears, when you look back on your life you see your failures and you fail because you make excuses. If you look into your excuses you'll find your deepest fears. For example:

- Can't find a significant other... it's because you fear rejection and thus don't reach out to people.
- Reason not to go to the gym and workout... afraid of not

fitting in or letting yourself down.
- Didn't ask for help... afraid of depending on someone who will inevitably let you down.
- Not going back to school as an adult... afraid of admitting to your own inadequacies.
- Won't leave your job or current significant other... afraid of leaving your comfort zone.
- Blaming others... afraid to examine yourself.

Fear leads to excuses which leads to failure. If you could do away with your fears you could turn your life around. The problem with that is you're not strong enough to rid yourself of your fears. If you were strong enough you would have done so by now.

You'll never be as cool as those you compare yourself too.

The first thing people do in the morning and the last thing they do in the evening is look at themselves in the mirror. Then throughout the day we compare ourselves to others. We watch beautiful and sexy people in television and movies. We follow the world most interesting man through his beer commercials and world most beautiful women on social media. Hell even our friends lives seem interesting by posting only the best part of their lives online. Why do we do this?

It's obvious you'll never be like the people you compare yourself to. You'll never be as cool-sexy-clever-innovative-good looking as they are. Maybe you can get your eyebrows to match that one Instagram star but your genetics will never match their natural born beauty. You will never be on a YouTube "People Are Awesome" video that features skilled adrenaline junkies and you'll never live the lavish lifestyle of the rich kids of Instagram.

Not all people are created equal, some people are indeed more valuable than others. Their value is shown in their beauty, wealth, and other attributes you compare with them. You may say "but my body's a temple, I was made in God's image." Let's be honest, the God you resemble is either Buda or Medusa.

You're replaceable.

We've established you have a unique set of imperfections but just because you're unique doesn't mean you're useful. What have you done with yourself? You eat too much junk, stay up too late, and you're slowly poisoning your body with alcohol, caffeine, and recreational/pharmaceutical drugs. You could offset some of these with a regimen of exercise and sleep but you don't even do that. Most people are in worse shape today than they were last week. We're a society of people slowly and unknowingly committing suicide and getting dumber over time.

You'll never find success.

First we need to define what success is. For the purpose of this book we'll use the only measure of success that matters, society's definition. Being successful is having an abundance of time, money, power, and followers. These are the things in life that matter and if you say they don't that only tells me that you don't have them. With that out of the way we establish a few basic premises.

If Olympic gold metal athletes, West Point graduates, and Presidents are capable of failure than you certainly are. Success and failure have nothing to do with hard work. Success has everything to do with luck and factors outside of our control or a well timed sex tape release, hence the Kardashians.

Unless you have a trump card you'll never become successful. When The Rock's football career failed he turned to wrestling which he was successful at, in part because his family was already firmly planted in the industry. He played his trump card, something you don't have. If you had one you would have exploited it by now.

Ch 5. You've been setting yourself up for failure.

Your goals, dreams, and aspirations are so bountiful that there's no other option but failure. It is better to want nothing and receive everything than to want everything and receive nothing.

Some of the happiest, most content people are Monks and hermits who aspire to a life of poverty, humility, and chastity. But you've never even considered renouncing your earthly pleasures in favor of a simpler life. Your ego wouldn't allow you to want so little though you know that it's your desires that have brought you nothing of actual value.

You annihilated your natural born instinct.

All your life you've processed cues from your environmental and social groups and combined that with millions of years of evolution to develop "instinct." For clarification this is the same instinct that lead you to believe that dating that crazy ex was a good idea, you know which one I'm talking about.

Your instinct has failed you your entire life because you've broke it. To you, instinct is something you've learned to manipulate to validate your sensitive feelings. It no longer has any real meaning in your life because instinct no longer comes from the gut but from your supposed intellect.

If you would have listened to your instinct you wouldn't have dated that crazy ex, it was your intellectual interpretation of your gut clouded by your minds feelings. Your mind can convince you of anything and it is not to be trusted.

Sowing the seeds of your demise.

The Bible says "As you sow, so shall you reap."

I added that in here for a fancy intro to say the only thing you've been sowing is the seeds to your own demise. Simply put, you don't work hard enough or on the right things. You have million dollar dreams but a minimum wage work ethic. You don't work hard enough, long enough, smart enough, and when you do it isn't on something that matters in relation to your goals, dreams, and aspirations. You put the ass in aspiration.

To settle down is to settle.

You've been preparing for a life of mediocrity since you could walk. It's actually so common that society coined a term for it, settling down. Common reasons for settling down as defined by society.

1. Taking a safe, boring job.
2. Settling for your current significant other.
3. You're so in debt you can no longer take

monitory risks.

    4.   Given up on your passions.

    5.   Trapped yourself by choosing to have kids.

To go off on a tangent, I say "choosing to have kids" because getting pregnant or getting someone pregnant isn't one of those things that happens by accident. People give excuses all the time for their "unplanned pregnancy" but deep down they wanted it (excluding rape of course).

That's why they chose not to use protection or switch to Plan B when the condom brakes. Most people will tell you they didn't notice the condom broke but that's because they knew if they checked they would have to face responsibility to chose to do something about it or not.

Misery loves company, that's why people want kids, to subject them to the same misery they've endured in this cold, dangerous, unforgiving world. So you left it up to chance, this way you can tell people it was an "accident" and that you're not ready to have kids. With this excuse in place less will be expected of you as a parent by society.

The excuse "I never thought it would happen to me" is complete BS. That line has been used for 3 million years back to when two sexually charged Homo Sapiens got it on in a cave on a woolly mammoth rug. They wanted a little cave baby rather than the responsibility of being the first to harness the power of fire or invent the wheel. They chose mediocrity as a way of life and when they told everyone they were settling down no one raised a monobrow.

Responsibility and excuses.

Ultimately the problem with being responsible is that responsibility breeds responsibility. For example the employees that I work with who are the most responsible are the most likely to be given more responsibilities. Being responsible isn't worth it if it's going to give you more work to do. This same thing can be said about dealing with your personal life.

Should you take responsibility for your life? Absolutely not! You're messed up with all your unresolved childhood issues, inner demons, and that minor Oedipus complex for your hot step mom. Life's easier when you decide not to take responsibility for it.

We all have cool things we want to do in our lives that we never get to doing. That's because we have to work for these things and for everything we want there's a quick excuse ready to make a counter argument.

Why don't we eat healthy? Because fast food is quicker/cheaper/tastier. Why don't we save money? Because spending it is enjoyable. Why do we gamble? Because risky investments are exciting. Why don't we get another degree? Because that would require acceptance of not being good enough.

If you make excuses to not pursue something it means you never really cared about it in the first place. And as for responsibility, stay away from it, it won't enrich your life.

Procrastination.

If there's something capable of being put off you'll put it off. It's inevitable and that's fine. You'll never amount to anything anyway so why try and change it. There's always time to do things later, it's not like you'll die any time soon. And with all the advancements in modern medicine you may live to 250 years old. The best way to live with procrastination is to own your particular brand of procrastination. To do that we'll need to identify what type of procrastinator you are.

1.   The Worrier type of procrastinator delays tasks as they discover the risks involved.

2.   The Perfectionist is someone who won't start a task until they know they can do it perfectly.

3.   The Day Dreamer is someone who, when faced with work, will shy away and think of something else.

4.   The Over-doer's are people who can't get things done because of the number of tasks they take on.

5.   The Defiant type will resist doing anything suggested by others so that they feel they have control of their life.

6.   The Distractors are people who will find other tasks to do rather than the important task at hand. For example; someone with an important test to study for will put it off because they feel they need to wash the dishes first.

7.   The Crisis Maker's wait till the last minute to do something.

8.   The List Maker's are so overly organized that they will postpone things as they make plans to get other things done.

9.   The Relaxed type of procrastinator will delay or blow off tasks for either self-indulgent reasons or fatigue.

We don't prescribe to one type 100% of the time but knowing the reason behind your procrastination will help you enjoy your time more. You can't rid yourself of procrastination and you wouldn't want to. Success is heavy and breeds responsibility. Not only is life much easier when you procrastinate but dreaming of someday being successful brings with it the joys of success without the work, fears, and heart ache of ultimately failing.

Ch 6. Hard Truths.

You can no longer hide from yourself what is expressed by your inner will. Your inner will has filled you with angst and left you with a reduction of morals and a rebellious attitude against the fundamental presuppositions of life. And yet you still possess your will. You've repeatedly concluded your distrust of humans, a hatred of animal nature, a longing for both materials and sensations, and yet you've retained your will all the same.

The one thing your will hasn't achieved yet is the compassion for nothing; to want nothing, need nothing, feel nothing. As Master Jedi Yoda once said, "Train yourself to let go of everything you fear to lose." There is still more accepting you must do within your soul before you achieve that nirvana and to get there you're going to have to accept some hard truths.

"The Pussy Generation"-Clint Eastwood

What makes you think blue collar jobs are beneath you? It's so apparent in my generation that they believe any type of skilled trade... let me rephrase that. It's so apparent in my generation that they believe any type of HARD WORK is a job for OTHER people.

Here's an example: It was the end of the day at the trampoline park and before we go home we have to clean the facility. I was divvying up tasks and told the new 17 year old employee to vacuum the platforms around the trampolines. His eyes widened and with all seriousness asked "Isn't that a job for other people?" Vacuuming is literally one of the easiest chores someone can do and this young punk thought it was beneath him.

I've also heard many people around my age complain how they can't find a job. Yet they would, on principle, never consider becoming a plumber, electrician, bridge builder, pipe fitter, cement worker, steel worker, HVAC specialist, refrigeration repairmen, general contractor, roofer, or welder.

Suddenly with the advent of technology based jobs these young adults believe that the jobs of their parents and parents' parents are in fact for old people or immigrants. And if you're a young girl saying those are man jobs well you need to stop contributing to the gender wage gap because these are high paying jobs.

There's a skilled welder shortage here in the US, by the end of 2015 there were 5.8 million job openings left unfilled in the welding trade. Starting off a new welder will make $30-40,000 in their first year. And for an underwater welder with no college education (or debt from going to college) will easily make over $100,000 for a few months deployment on an oil rig.

Yes being a skilled tradesman is hard work and you'll earn every dollar of that but it's a recession proof job. You'll never be laid off, you'll have more work than you can handle (which means you can charge a premium), and you'll put food on the table every night for your family. Or ditch the family and buy a new sports car every year, the choice is yours.

What more do you want? Oh, that's right. You want to sit on your butt collecting welfare checks more than you want to be successful. And when you do look for a job you look to be an easily replaceable "team member" putting square blocks in square holes for minimum wage while you dream about becoming a Youtube superstar or Instafamous all the while pushing for a higher minimum wage because you know your dreams won't come true. So the next time you feel underpaid know that you're not, you're under skilled and you need to accept that you're a pussy.

Ch-ch-ch-changes.

On the subject of change a behaviorist will tell you that all you need to change is a change of environment. But most psychologists would disagree sighting the importance of history and internal dynamics. Sigmund Freud who founded psychoanalysis felt one aspect of our actions stem from thoughts and feelings buried deep with in us, unbeknownst to our conscious selves. Freudians argue that these thoughts and feelings are repressed motives. You see, deep down we're all driven by our subconsciousness.

This begs the question what lies in our subconsciousness, and the answer may disturb you. Our subconsciousness is filled with weird sexual desires forbidden in society, aggressive urges to harm others and ourselves, as well as repressed anti social tendencies.

These aren't things you can change, only repress. As a functioning member of society (and I use that phrase lightly) you've probably developed some strong defenses to keep these hidden from yourself and the world.

But should you ever want to change? I argue, no, better the devil you know over the devil you don't. At least you know how to deal with your current life as you've grown accustomed to your worthlessness. Building off of that, change is scary! To gain something means you'll have to lose something, that's just physics. And this will involve death, illness, tragedy; losses of all kinds.

Some changes are inevitable and we'll discuss strategies and tactics in how to deal with change in Chapter 9. But first we'll discuss the subject of changing yourself in the next chapter if it's even possible.

Accepting failure into your life.

Much has been revealed about how students in the United States test so poorly compared to other first world countries. And inevitably during a Q&A of every presidential debate someone will ask the nominees what they'll do to fix this. But the solution doesn't involve increased spending, school uniforms, or better training/higher wages for teachers.

The cold hard truth is that students only learn when they want to learn and they're only successful when they want to be successful. Getting good grades is a choice, a choice made to work hard and be successful. So why aren't students choosing to be successful in school when they know there's a direct correlation to how one does after graduation?

These students will tell you to your face that they want success and they think they do because they believe the excuses they tell themselves about why they are doing poorly. "The wrong material was on the study guide," "too busy to study the night before," "distractions in the classroom," or "the teacher is bad." Whatever the excuse they use they always come out as the innocent victim.

These students say they want success when in reality all their actions are motivated towards failure, which leaves 2 options for how to move forward after acknowledging your own hypocrisy.

1. Choose to be successful.
2. Accept the failure.

You've already made your choice and you've been choosing to accept failure every day of your life. And in this most unlikely of places I'm going to tell you that's alright. Failure has taken a negative connotation in todays society but there's an allure to failure just like there are trappings to success.

Once you've begun succeeding in life others will begin to expect success from you and that expectation can be more crippling than the fear of failure. Success also makes you appear to be a threat to others and this is the reason why female valedictorians have such a high droop out rate when they get to college. That's not me being mean, it's the truth. The reason so many intelligent women drop out of college is because they want acceptance and that's not something they can receive when they're perceived as an educational threat.

Living with worthlessness.

We've established you're a worthless low achiever and rather than work at becoming one of those "try hards" you can take steps to be happy as a low achiever. This way you can also fight the unfair social norms. Hurray Social Justice Warriors!

1. Avoid tasks related to success that you're not good at.

2. Give up when work gets hard, put it off, and do something meaningless.

3. Only choose tasks with a 100% success rate, as to improve your self esteem.

4. Curb your expectations, you won't be working hard with your typical low energy anyway.

5. Put as much blame on others and situational aspects as possible to avoid taking responsibilities for yourself and actions.

6. Find humility in your failure and you'll be fine. This leads us to Chapter 7 and I think you'll like it.

Ch 7. The plan of inaction.

You've been fighting your worthlessness your whole life and it's gotten you nowhere. Failure has crept into your life because you've been living in denial. Whenever something negative happens you perceive yourself as the victim, the truth is you've brought all that negativity into your life. But you're not a victim, the reason you fail is because you're inauthentic.

Being authentic is about acting as one's self, not as one acts. For example when you give money to the homeless you think you're a good person but the action of giving doesn't mean you're authentically good. The authentic thing to do in a situation like that is to search your soul for how that person makes you feel then act on the feeling. Instead of pretending to feel sympathy your authentic response could be to tell that person that they stink, they're taking up too much room on the sidewalk, or that they should go get a job to be miserable like the rest of us.

As for where worthlessness is concerned you need to act on that because you're worthless. To try and remove worthlessness from your life is inauthentic. Right now you're the best you'll ever be, it's not what you want to hear but it's the truth. Own your worthlessness, don't try and hide it, it's the only way you'll find freedom.

It's time for a new plan. The days of trying to better your life are over and it's time for you to accept your worthlessness. From here on you need to implement a series of inactions to combat the fallacy that you can be better than who you are.

Don't bother trying to change.

I'd like to take this opportunity to talk about change and why trying to get rid of your worthlessness isn't only difficult it's impossible. Take body weight for example, you have what scientists refer to as "biological destiny." Your body works to maintain it's weight and does so by adjusting your metabolism and through food cravings.

For example if you start a diet and begin eating less your metabolism will slow down and your cravings for sweets and fats will increase resulting in you maintaining your weight. Losing weight is also made difficult as people become emotionally attached to food and the heavier you are the more insulin your body produces when you see food which creates hunger pains. It's a vicious cycle.

But if you think changing your body weight is difficult try getting off an addiction to drugs. The relapse rate of those trying to get off their addiction is so high that 2/3rds to 3/4ths relapse within 3 months.

Subconsciously you don't even want to change. You crave sleeping in and loathe people who show up early to everything. And if you don't like doing chores that's okay, humans aren't born with the need to wash dishes or vacuum the carpet. It would be great if we were, but we're not. You're born with the need to eat, sleep, and have loud, hot, passionate, sweaty, unprotected sex 'til the early hours of the morning with a young tattoo artist you just met off of Craigslist, while your neighbor Tim/Tom pounds on the wall yelling that he's trying to sleep.

Changing who you are is impossible and there will always be something to hold you back whether it's biology, your chemical makeup, or years of bad decisions forming habits. Just be yourself, worthlessness and all, it's the only thing you're good at.

The malfeasance of self confidence.

When developing a plan of inaction it's important not to build self confidence as that will hinder the process. When you have self confidence you feel good and when you feel good you're setting yourself up to feel bad later. Happiness is sadness that hasn't happened yet.

Here are five simple and easy steps you can follow to avoid self confidence.

1. Understand that you're not responsible. Responsibility breeds responsibility and you want to avoid that at all costs.

2. Understand that you're not in control and therefore not capable of directing your life.

3. Don't accumulate skill sets. A skill set is

like owning a truck, every time your friends need to move something big and heavy they'll call you because you own a truck.

    4.   Avoid learning.

    5.   Play it safe and make excuses whenever possible.

Your ego is the root of all your suffering so you need to learn humility and strip yourself of all your self confidence. Monks don't feel pain only because they don't feel pleasure. If you're serious about being able to live with yourself you must be able to live with your worthlessness.

Hakuna Matata.

The Disney movie <u>The Lion King</u> is about a obnoxious privileged lion cub named Simba who can't wait for his good ole dad's death or ostracization (traditionally done by trail by combat by the son or rival male lion). This way he can become King as featured in the song <u>I Just Can't Wait to be King.</u>

Wanting to be King, Simba sets in motion a series of events that leads to his fathers death and he immediately regrets this decision. Now he faced with responsibilities for the first time in his life. He takes the right action by running away from his problems and yet he is still confused and conflicted. This is the part in the hero's journey when he meets the wise elders who set him straight, in this case Timon and Pumbaa.

>Timon: (talking about Simba) Gee. He looks blue.
>
>Pumbaa: I'd say brownish-gold.
>
>Timon: No, no, no, I mean he's depressed.
>
>Pumbaa: Oh. (talking to Simba) Hey kid, what's eatin' ya?
>
>Timon: Nothing; he's at the top of the food chain! (laughs hysterically) The food chain! (sees no reaction from Pumbaa or Simba) So... where're ya from?
>
>Simba: Who cares? I can't go back.
>
>Timon: Aaaaaah, you're an outcast. That's great, so are we!
>
>Pumbaa: What did you do, kid?
>
>Simba: Something terrible. I don't want to talk about it.
>
>Timon: Good, we don't wanna hear about it!
>
>Pumbaa: Come on, Timon. (to Simba) Anything we can do?
>
>Simba: Not unless you can change the past.
>
>Pumbaa: (trying to cheer him up) Kid, at times like this, my buddy Timon here says "You gotta put your behind in your

past!"--

    Timon: No, no no!

    Pumbaa: I mean--

    Timon: Amateur. Lie down, before you hurt yourself. (to Simba) It's "You gotta put your past behind you." Look, kid, bad things happen, and you can't do anything about it, right?

    Simba: Right.

    Timon: WRONG! "When the world turns its back on you, you turn your back on the world!"

    Simba: Well, that's not what I was taught.

    Timon: Then maybe you need a new lesson...

    Disney hit the nail on the head here because if you would ask anyone else they'll tell you that you need to take responsibility for your actions. But what they are really asking you to do is not put the responsibility on them. Because once you take ownership of your problems they no longer have to deal with it and it's up to you to do something or not. When you find you have no one to blame but yourself, do what Simba and his new pals did, turn around, protect your ego, and sing Hakuna Matata as you dance away.

Finalizing change.

We discussed the option of not bothering to change yourself but we can't control the things that change around us. This brings up the final question of how do you deal with change when it comes roaring into your life? The answer is to treat it the same as your responsibilities and ignore it.

One thing my dad always says is "It's always something." Maybe the tire is flat, the grill stopped working, the dog needs to go to the vet, a tornado just touched down two blocks over, "It's always something." So why not ignore as much as possible? It's what everyone else is doing. At the time of me writing this, the Republicans and Democrats are angry at each other (go figure). Republicans are upset that a football player isn't standing for the National Anthem and the Democrats are upset that one of President Trump's councilors had her feet on the couch in the Oval Office. Someone should probably be talking about how the country is almost 20,000,000,000,000 in debt, but hey it's not my problem.

I know what you're saying, "But Mr. All Knowing Author Man, not all change can be ignored." Well listen up young grasshopper, if you change the way you look at things, the things you look at change. Rather than believe your expulsion from school was a bad thing, think of it as saving tens of thousands on student loan debt then cowboy up and start a career in welding. Didn't get that promotion you wanted at work? Good, take this opportunity to sit on the couch and catch up on the video games you've been neglecting. Change can't be stopped but you'll always have control of how you react to it.

Ch 8. Things to remember on your journey nowhere.

Life is tough. It's a struggle and you're not strong enough to meet it's challengers head-on while being a productive member of society. I don't want you to give up on life, but rather, find alternate outlets for your weak will. Over the final three chapters we will discuss things such as developing bad tastes and bad habits on purpose because this will add some sense of control in your life.

Sometimes we get caught up in the troubles of life. A person can feel the weight of the world on their shoulders as if to bear the suffering of others. We're not Jesus, that's not our cross to bear and we shouldn't have to carry the weight of anything except for our own worthlessness.

The Hierarchy of Needs.

If you're not going to go anywhere in life there's no reason to concern yourself with the higher functions of humanity. Don't worry about climate change, the destruction of the worlds rain forest, or finding a purpose in life. Be minimalist in your approach to life and focus on your basic needs.

There's in fact a hierarchy of needs and the idea is that before you can satisfy the higher needs of humanity you must first satisfy the lower ones.

1. Biological and physiological needs: air, water, food, sleep, shelter, sex.
2. Safety needs: physical safety, physical security, law and order.
3. Belonging and love needs: friendship, intimacy, trust, acceptance,and being part of a social group.
4. Self-esteem needs: to feel competent, respected, and worthwhile, as well as reaching a level independence and success.

5. Self-actualization needs: reaching fulfillment through growth, gaining the wisdom to understand oneself/others, and finding a purpose in life.

So if you're not having sex then you're not even meeting level one on the hierarchy of needs. And that's not me talking, that's modern psychology telling you that you're worthless. Shedding your worthlessness doesn't come until you're at least on level 4. The importance of knowing where you lie on the hierarchy of needs is so you can relieve yourself of the more complex problems facing humanity.

The indifference of the universe.

You'll work your whole life and have only the tinniest impact on the world in the smallest sliver of the existence of time. There's 8 planets in our solar system and more than 500 known solar systems in our galaxy. And our galaxy is one of 700,000,000,000,000,000,000,000 (700 sextillion) in the universe as estimated by NASA. I'll let you do the math on how many planets are in the universe. Knowing that do you think you really matter in the grand scheme of things?

In this way the universe is liken to the honey badger. Honey badger don't care, honey badger don't give a sh*t. Do you think of yourself as a King Cobra? Honey badger chase you up a tree and eat you anyway. You can inject it with your venom from your fangs which would kill a rhino but not the honey badger, he'll just take a little nap then wake up and continue eating you because he's a hungry little bastard.

An entire colony of killer bees work tirelessly to make honey to feed and house larva, honey badger gonna come eat it, larva and all. The bee's will sting it until their little stingers fall off their butts but the honey badger is hungry. It doesn't care about being stung, nothing can stop the honey badger when it's hungry. They don't have any regard for anything, you could be a mouse or a pride of lions, honey badger don't give a f#ck and neither does the universe.

Sh*t Happens.

Often when someone is about to do something incredibly stupid there will be someone else encouraging them saying "Go big or go home." That statement should be a clear indicator that you shouldn't do whatever you were about to do and go home. Let's be honest you'd probably rather take a nap anyway.

The reason why you should go home is because sh*t happens and that doubly applies when stupid decisions are being made and quadruples when you're drunk. Murphie's law is an adage that is stated as: Anything that can go wrong, will go wrong. Trust me it will go wrong.

So the next time someone tells you to "Go big or go home," and you decide to go big and it turns out you broke your leg, two things are going to happen. First is that I'm going to say I told you so and the second one is what you should do about it.

Be silent, morose, and bad tempered out of annoyance and disappointment. That's right I'm telling you to sulk. Sulking feels amazing. It tells everyone exactly how you feel without having to speak and it gives you the attention you craved in the first place when you decided to go big. So congratulations, I guess?

It's too late to die young.

The best advice I ever heard my father give was to my 12 year old impressionable cousin. He said, "Never get old, die young." I was too young at the time to understand but now that I'm older I see the wisdom in his words. I would have liked to pass on this advice to you but it's too late.

If you're reading this, it's because you've already lost your innocence and therefore it's too late to die young. There's no longer any point to ending your life, to have died without knowing the tragedies and sorrows of life would have been nice but you and I have passed that point. We might as well stick it out and suck what pleasure we can out of the remainder of our lives. Just give meaning to your suffering and move on.

Your life belongs to you, so do whatever you want. If making what's traditionally considered "bad" decisions are the decisions that bring excitement to your life continue to do them despite what others tell you. Don't let anyone tell you can't be happy or that you should be happy in the way they're happy. This leads us to Chapter 9.

Ch 9. Do whatever you want.

Rid yourself of the responsibility of morality because the more you struggle to be perfect in the eyes of yourself and others the more sickness you'll put yourself through. Our morality is what separates us from the animals but morality is also what induces self-torture. Because we are so inward looking we are constantly at odds with our animalistic roots and thus we struggle against our nature.

Most people don't realize it but they delight in affirming their suffering by choosing to be moral. They view the dismissal of our animalistic and evolutionary past as triumphs rather than the torments that they are. But not everyone is strong enough to take on this suffering.

Many people who harm themselves, directly or indirectly, do so because they are overwhelmed with the sickness that is morality and the constant desire to be perfect. In order to regain your health you must let go of these ideals.

Once you've freed yourself you can then assert your own ideals and desires that are in accordance with your will in order to live out an authentic and happy life.

Predestination.

There was a religious movement during the mid 1500's called Calvinism in which it's followers believed God had predetermined who he'd take with him to Heaven before the world was created. Furthermore they believed that the chosen "elect" couldn't lose their salvation.

How would you behave if you believed you could do no wrong? I can't think of anything more freeing, that any choice I made was okay in the eyes of the Almighty. Under this philosophy absolutely nothing is off limits because life doesn't even matter, we're just here for the ride waiting for eternal damnation or salvation.

If your life doesn't matter then your choices don't as well, understanding that eliminates decision fatigue when it comes to life's many questions. So do what you want, be who you want to be, and take what you want. I'm not saying do deplorable stuff but I'm not saying you shouldn't either.

Reward Yourself.

Rewards feel awesome, there's no two ways about it. The problem is we're only rewarded for good things and when we do bad things we're punished. Where did these rules come from? Why shouldn't we be able to reward ourselves for when we do bad things?

Choosing to act on bad decisions is one of the more pleasurable and exciting things in life. Great stories never begin with the sentence, "after I finish my salad." No they begin with, "hold my beer." Bad decisions make great memories and are hilarious when we look back on them.

Society tells us to be perfect angels and to not make bad decisions. But if you're like me you don't remember the nights where you went to bed on time. It's the nights where you stayed up late with God knows who doing God knows what. Those are the moments you'll giggle about when you're in a nursing home in your 90's and those are the decisions you should reward yourself for.

Take control of your life.

Unlike bad decisions made one at a time, habits tend to last forever. It's difficult to get rid of a bad habit and it's as tough to form a new good habit. Because of this we're just going to ignore both of those.

The only way for you to take control of your life is to purposely develop new bad habits. This should be a lot of fun as you can pick from literally thousands of bad habits including but not limited to; codependency, obsessive compulsive disorders, sexual addiction, caffeine addiction, drug addiction, compulsive spending, compulsive eating or an eating disorder, gambling, nail biting, bedwetting, porn addiction, smoking, and on and on.

What's most important is feeling good and it feels good to have control of your life which you'll have once you're able to control the input of habits. Not to mention most of these bad habits feel good while you do them. They relieve stress and anxiety which may be more beneficial to you than doing away with the bad habits and holding on to those negative feelings.

Effort is discomfort.

Life wants to do things the easiest way possible for the biggest payout. Trees that are planted along side roads in urban centers never look healthy because they have to work so hard. They deal with pollution, dog piss on their trunks, and their root system has to fight with concrete for space while it's branches are overly trimmed. Fruit trees in these positions never produce much and when they do it's low quality fruit.

The same thing goes for your life. The more effort you have to put into staying alive the less you'll enjoy being alive. It's science and it's part of what's called the law of least effort.

The law of least effort is about following the path of least resistance for the greatest amount of harmony. It covers everything from botany to evolutionary biology and it's something you can apply to your life .

Outsource your work. This is what you're doing when you're ordering a pizza. You call up your favorite pizza place, tell them to make you food, and they deliver it to your door. It costs a couple bucks more than making your own pizza and the benefits include staying in your comfy home doing whatever it was you were doing before you got hungry. The same goes for mowing your lawn. The cost of a good lawnmower and gas is the same as paying the neighbor's kid to cut your grass for a year. All this without the discomfort of working hard.

    Outsourcing your work is different from being lazy, it's being smart. Mowing the lawn is hard, sweaty monotonous work so have someone else do it. Whenever you're faced with having to do work the first thing you should do is see if there's someone else you can have do it because their effort is your comfort.

Effort is discomfort.

Life wants to do things the easiest way possible for the biggest payout. Trees that are planted along side roads in urban centers never look healthy because they have to work so hard. They deal with pollution, dog piss on their trunks, and their root system has to fight with concrete for space while it's branches are overly trimmed. Fruit trees in these positions never produce much and when they do it's low quality fruit.

The same thing goes for your life. The more effort you have to put into staying alive the less you'll enjoy being alive. It's science and it's part of what's called the law of least effort.

The law of least effort is about following the path of least resistance for the greatest amount of harmony. It covers everything from botany to evolutionary biology and it's something you can apply to your life .

Outsource your work. This is what you're doing when you're ordering a pizza. You call up your favorite pizza place, tell them to make you food, and they deliver it to your door. It costs a couple bucks more than making your own pizza and the benefits include staying in your comfy home doing whatever it was you were doing before you got hungry. The same goes for mowing your lawn. The cost of a good lawnmower and gas is the same as paying the neighbor's kid to cut your grass for a year. All this without the discomfort of working hard.

Outsourcing your work is different from being lazy, it's being smart. Mowing the lawn is hard, sweaty monotonous work so have someone else do it. Whenever you're faced with having to do work the first thing you should do is see if there's someone else you can have do it because their effort is your comfort.

Ch 10. Taming your life.

No matter how hard you try you'll never be able to put a square peg into a round hole without destroying something in the process. And in case you haven't been paying attention, the same applies to your life. Fighting against your will has brought nothing but destruction.

The key to your salvation is in your hands. Your desires only serve as anchors, free yourself of them and find enlightenment in the emptiness. Through enlightenment there's no ego, no pain, no suffering. Once you've freed yourself you can flow in accordance with your will and live an authentic life.

Bruce Lee had this to say on the subject, "You must be shapeless, formless, like water. When you pour water in a cup, it becomes the cup. When you pour water in a bottle, it becomes the bottle. When you pour water in a teapot, it becomes the teapot. Water can drip and it can crash. Become like water my friend."

What he's talking about is finding harmony in living authentically through one's will. Accept your worthlessness. We are worthless and there's no running from it so own it. The best we can do is live in harmony with our worthlessness.

Strategy Vs Tactics.

Let me throw in some military lingo from back in my Call of Duty days. Here in Strategy vs Tactics we won't be discussing something to directly implement into your life as the other sections of this chapter will, this is about you having the vocabulary to better orchestrate your life.

In life you will always arrive at your destination. So far in life you probably haven't had a destination in mind and it's led you here to the middle of nowhere. If your destination is nowhere that's exactly where you will end up. You're going to have to change your mindset and pursue a specific destination if you're going to have a chance at getting to where you want to go.

To do this you'll have to implement strategy and

tactics. Strategy is the art of planning and directing the operations and movements of your life to reach an objective. Tactics are the implementation of actions used to reach an objective that was laid out by the strategy. You need both. Most people tend to be more tactically oriented, they do ten different things with no real direction or purpose in mind which gets them nowhere.

Here's an example of how to properly use strategy and tactics. A U.S Navy Seal may adopt the objective of being the hardest person on Earth to kill. Their strategy could be something along the lines of planning and directing their life so that they become stronger mentally and physically. The tactics could include rigorous physical training along with training in the necessary skill set's required to keep them alive in adverse conditions (combat). And they could also include taking extreme ownership of their life while putting their ego in check as to not be blinded by their pride.

Be as successful as you want to be.

Part of taking control of our lives is about not giving into the ideals of others. Your family wants you to be the most successful person on the planet. If your parents had a strategy for you growing up it would be to give you everything you needed to be the most successful person in history. But it's on you to decide what you'll do with your potential.

The people in your life, not just your family, will push you towards their idea of success but they only know what's best for them. They will push you and the more they push the more you'll resist, that's just human nature. If you don't establish the type and amount of success that works for you they will beat you down with their pushing.

So take a hard look at your life, independent from the opinions of others. You'll notice you probably don't even want success. Most people just want to be left alone and enjoy a football game with friends on the weekends. And if you do find you want modest success it certainly won't be what your friends and family had in mind for you. If that's the case then develop a strategy and employ the tactics necessary to be successful.

Procrastination.

In Chapter 5 we established the 9 different types of procrastination; the worrier, the perfectionist, the day dreamer, the over-doer, the defiant type, the distractor, the crisis maker, the list maker, and the relaxed type. This was to help you identify the top ways you procrastinate, now let's take that information and utilize it. Chances are you've used two to three types for most of your procrastination.

If you want to turn your life around you're going to have to modify a few things and this is one of them. Procrastination is impossible to eliminate so let's change the way we do it. Experiment with the other 7 or so types of procrastination that you rarely engage in. So the next time you find yourself procrastinating through day dreaming switch things up and start worrying about the task at hand and see how that affects you and your life. You can't change, but at least you can try new things, who knows what the results will uncover.

Unmotivated Motivation.

If you recall back in Chapter 3. we discussed how motivation is counter evolutionary. That's still true, you've evolved in such a way to keep you from wanting to potentially put yourself in a compromising position. This is why being motivated is so rare and you'll typically find when you have motivation it's motivation to do something at a later time. That's because you're thinking of the rewards but when you're faced with actually having to perform the action the motivation will be nowhere to be found.

When the time comes you know what you need to do but if you think about doing anything long enough you'll undoubtedly decide not to do it. Hesitation is what tells the brain that the next action will either be calorie expensive, dangerous, or unpleasant. Once hesitation begins your brain will immediately begin coming up with excuses on why you don't feel like doing it.

There's no waiting to be motivated, if you wait till you feel like doing something you'll never get it done. So when a task comes up you need to decide that moment if you want to either be miserable but get something done or be comfortable and accomplish nothing.

Essentially what you're doing by acting without the motivation to act is perusing future high grade happiness. You're sacrificing your current comfort for something which may benefit you down the road. So if that's the route you want to take all you have to do is act before the hesitation can begin.

When you know you have to do something start counting down immediately, 3, 2, 1 and go into action. Waiting any longer than that and you'll only be met with hesitation and excuses.

Laugh

I took a public speaking class in college and for the final we had to give a presentation in front of the whole class. The guidelines were such that we could pick any topic we wanted but the goal was to convince our classmates of something in five minutes. Being millennial, college educated snowflakes the students picked topics such as:

Why you should vote democrat.
Why violence shouldn't exists.
Why the government should pay for our education.
Why (enter any group) are oppressed.
Why you should save the whales.

The list went on and on and it was the most boring four hours of my life as each student spouted off the snowflake agenda and whatnot. I had been the last person to sign up with a topic so I went last. By this point my classmates were mostly asleep when I uploaded my power point presentation and took to the podium.

The first slide came up and read, "Why you should watch stand up comedy on YouTube." You see, laughter releases stress and stress hinders performance. There's literally tens of thousands of stand up routines on YouTube for your enjoyment and betterment.

There are jokes for every topic you could think of. Political jokes, practical jokes, pirate jokes, penis jokes, parenting jokes, patient jokes, pregnancy jokes, pickle jokes, and those are just jokes that start with P.

I didn't even have time to mention the countless hours of YouTube videos dedicated to Epic Fails where you can sit back and laugh at the misery of others, which feels amazing in it's own right. So the next time you're feeling stressed or are ignoring the pile of work you need to do, fire up the internet and head over to YouTube. You'll be glad you did.

*The Most Important Lesson In

This Book*

    Someone once said "In life there are no failures or mistakes, only opportunities for growth." This person obviously never called out the wrong name while having sex. Humans are perfectly capable of complete and utter irredeemable failure. You and I are living proof of that but that doesn't mean we can't live happy lives. We'll never be as rich as Bill Gates, as famous as Kim Kardashian, or have the power of a King but we will have more character, our failures have given us that much.

    Accept yourself for the worthless person you are, go fourth, make mistakes, and be deplorable. But most importantly of all, feel good and look cool while you do it because that's all that really matters.

In Conclusion

    Having read this book I hope you'll walk away, not with a sense of self-hatred, but rather a sense of peace. You were never going to amount to anything so don't be upset with yourself when you don't achieve greatness. Don't stress over the fact that you're worthless because that's just the way it is. You're the person you're meant to be, worthlessness and all.

    So the next time you look at yourself in the mirror, know that you're worthless and that your life has no meaning but smile anyway. Accept yourself for who you are and own that identity. If you can't find harmony with yourself then at least take some pleasure in knowing that there's probably someone on the planet more worthless than you, that's my final lesson.

    If you're upset with me for calling you out on your

worthlessness then check out my other books. <u>I'm Worthless And I Know It Volumes 1 and 2</u>. They feature multiple short stories from my life that depict what a worthless individual I am.

    Like you, I've struggled with worthlessness all my life and these dark comedies feature my most embarrassing and regretful moments that you're sure to find pleasure in. Like the time I fell in love with two girls that turned out to be in a relationship with each other. And the time when I figured out that the vagina and anus where two separate holes (oh and I was 17 years old when I finally figured that one out). I've discovered my specific brand of worthlessness and I hope you'll enjoy yourself at my expense.

    Break a leg,

    Will Jorden

Printed in Great Britain
by Amazon